FERNHURST|BOOKS

T0364386

9 781898 660804

waterproof
notebook
pocket-sized

Suitable for most writing and drawing tools. For multiple use, a pencil
and rubber are recommended. A larger lined version is also available.

FERNHURST|BOOKS

Fernhurst Books Limited
The Windmill
Mill Lane
Harbury
Leamington Spa
Warwickshire
CV33 9HP
UK
Tel: +44 (0) 1926 337488
www.fernhurstbooks.com

£5.99

ISBN 978-1898-66080-4

9 781898 660804